SPOTLIGHT ON SOCCER

TEAMWORK IN SOCCER

Clive Gifford

PowerKiDS press

New York

Published in 2011 by The Rosen Publishing Group Inc.
29 East 21st Street, New York, NY 10010

First Edition

Editor: Julia Adams
Produced by: Tall Tree Ltd.
Editor, Tall Tree: Jon Richards
Designer: Ben Ruocco

Library of Congress Cataloging-in-Publication Data

Gifford, Clive.
  Teamwork in soccer / Clive Gifford. -- 1st ed.
      p. cm. -- (Spotlight on soccer)
  Includes index.
  ISBN 978-1-61532-609-9 (library binding)
  ISBN 978-1-61532-614-3 (paperback)
  ISBN 978-1-61532-618-1 (6-pack)
  1. Soccer--Juvenile literature. 2. Teamwork (Sports)--
Juvenile literature. I. Title.
  GV943.25.G554 2011
  796.334'2--dc22

                                          2009045765

Photographs
All photographs taken by Michael Wicks, except;
t—top, l—left, r—right, b—bottom, c—center
cover t—Dreamstime.com/Val_th, tr—Dreamstime.com/
Sebcz, br—Dreamstime.com/Val_th, bl—Dreamstime.
com/Spartak, tl—Michael Wicks, c—Dreamstime.
com/Katseyephoto, 2 Dreamstime.com/Mitchell
Gunn, 4 Andres Kudacki/Corbis, 8 Dreamstime.com/
Mitchell Gunn, 16 Gilbert Iundt/TempSport/Corbis,
17b Dreamstime.com/Mitchell Gunn, 24 Greg Fiume/
NewSport/Corbis, 25 Dreamstime.com/Susana Carvalho,
26br Matthew Ashton/AMA/Corbis, 27 Sampics/Corbis,
30 Ben Radford/Corbis, 32 Dreamstime.com/Susana
Carvalho

Acknowledgements
The author and publisher would like to thank the
following people for their help and participation in this
book: Whiteknights FC, Eric Burrow, Steve Rendell, and
Paul Scholey.

Manufactured in China.
CPSIA Compliance Information: Batch #WAS0102PK: For Further Information contact
Rosen Publishing, New York, New York at 1-800-237-9932

CONTENTS

The Team Game

Soccer is an action-packed team sport that pits two sides, each containing 11 players, against each other. The players control, pass, and run with the ball with the aim of scoring goals.

Working Together

Throughout the world of soccer, there are plenty of cases of players from supposedly weaker teams using good tactics and working well together to beat teams full of superstars. For example, even though the England team consisted of many superstar players, such as Steven Gerrard, they lost games and failed to qualify for the Euro 2008 tournament. There are plenty of examples of teams beaten by supposedly lesser teams—a feat known as giant-killing. In Euro 2004, nobody thought Greece would win, but by working together, the team won the trophy by beating Portugal, Spain, and France.

At Euro 2008, Spain combined a team full of superstars, such as Fernando Torres, with good tactics and teamwork to win the tournament.

Plenty of practice in small, five-a-side games will help to improve teamwork and coordination and turn a group of individuals into a well-organized unit.

Individuals and Teams

Although players need excellent individual skills, soccer is a team game. The media (newspapers, television, radio, and the Internet) often focus on a star individual in a team, such as the team's most skillful winger or its most successful goal scorer. These players may be game changers, but without the support and good play of the rest of their team, they are unlikely to shine. How a team is organized and how the players choose to attack and defend are known as tactics. These are usually decided on by the team's coach or manager.

> **I've never considered one player to be all-important. In football [soccer], you win or lose together as a team.**
>
> Italian striker,
> **Alessandro Del Piero**

Training and the Team

Working well as a team takes hours of training. Although training is essential to improve each player's own skills, it is also where players get to know each other's strengths and weaknesses.

Types of Training

Players train regularly, beginning with a warm-up and a series of muscle stretches. They then take part in a series of drills and games designed to sharpen their speed, skills, and awareness. All the time, the players learn more about how their teammates run, which foot they prefer to use, and how good they are at heading the ball. Teams often play a lot of training games, such as five-a-side. These games help players communicate with each other and build partnerships on the field.

Tactics Tip

Do not try to hurry your warm-up. Take your time to stretch your muscles and build up your heart rate steadily. If you try to do too much too quickly, you could injure yourself.

Warming Up

1 Warming up should start with gentle jogging. This raises the players' heart rate and gradually warms up their muscles.

2 Jogging should be followed by gentle stretching. Here, the players are stretching the hamstring muscles at the backs of their legs.

3 After stretching, players can start some more strenuous exercise to raise the heart rate even more, such as sprints, as these players are doing.

Watching Players

Coaches watch training closely. How the players train can have a major influence on who the coaches select to play and what tactics they choose for their teams. For example, a star player may look tired in training, and this might force the coach to not play them in the next match or to put them on the substitute's bench. The coach may also discover that someone is capable of playing in more than one position. If the team is hit by injuries, the coach may try this player out in a new position.

> **Failure happens all the time. It happens every day in practice. What makes you better is how you react to it.**
>
> United States women's team record goal scorer, **Mia Hamm**

These players are taking part in a simple training routine called a one-touch triangle. They stand in a triangle and pass the ball quickly between each other using just one touch. This helps the players develop their passing skills with both feet, and it also helps their teammates spot which foot they favor.

Decision Makers

Coaches and managers are the people in charge of soccer teams. Managers are involved in some of the business of a club, such as buying and selling players. Coaches are involved just in training players for the matches.

Making Decisions

Coaches and managers have a squad of players from which they can select a team to start a match. They will base their decisions on the tactics they want to use and the strengths of their available players. Sometimes, a coach or manager will risk the anger of fans to drop a star player who is tired or playing badly. Spanish coach José Luis Aragones did not take striker Raul to Euro 2008, a move that outraged some fans. However, Spain went on to win the competition.

Sir Alex Ferguson is one of the most successful managers in the world. In more than 20 years in charge at Manchester United, he has won nine Premier League titles and two Champions League crowns.

Prematch Briefing

Players discuss tactics and listen to their coach's briefing before a match. This is when the coach tells his players what tactics they should use during the game. However, there should be another plan if the original one does not work.

Tactics Tip

Listen carefully to your coach's prematch briefing, but do not be afraid to say if the plan is not working during a match. Sometimes, the players are better placed to see what is happening on the field.

Scouting Opponents

At the top level, coaches and managers study their upcoming opponents carefully. They attend matches, send assistants to scout the opponents, and watch recorded matches on computers or DVD. All the time, they are looking for weaknesses and how their own team might exploit them. In 2007, for instance, Croatia's coach, Slaven Bilic, used tactics to attack and isolate England's injury-hit defense, which contained new players. His team recorded a famous 2–1 victory at Wembley and subsequently qualified for Euro 2008.

Formations

Teams are made up of a goalkeeper and three basic types of outfield player called defenders, midfielders, and strikers or attackers. How these players line up to start a game is called a team's formation.

A wingback (in blue) surges forward with the ball at his feet to start an attack. Wingbacks play mainly along the flanks of the field.

Playing Positions

Defenders are responsible for stopping the opposition scoring goals. They tend to be good at heading the ball away and strong in the tackle. Fullbacks are defenders who play closer to the sidelines. Midfielders help in both defense and attack. They cover a lot of ground during a game. Midfielders who play out near the sidelines are known as wingers. These are attack-minded players whose aim is to beat defenders and shoot or pass to a teammate. Teams play with one, two, or occasionally, three strikers. These are a team's strongest goal scorers and tend to play closest to the opponent's goal.

Team Structure

Playing formations are expressed as numbers in rows of defenders, midfielders, and attackers. For example, a 4-4-2 formation means four defenders, four midfielders, and two strikers. Formations can be more complicated with one player playing behind a single striker (4-4-1-1), or a midfield anchor playing just in front of the defense (4-1-3-2). Another popular formation today is 3-5-2, with the two players called wingbacks, on the flanks of the five-man midfield.

ON THE BALL

In 1872, England used a 1-1-8 formation with eight attackers in a match against Scotland. Even so, the game finished 0–0.

4-4-1-1 Formation

This formation sees four players in defense, with two playing in the center and one fullback on each side. The supporting striker acts as a link between the midfielders and the front striker.

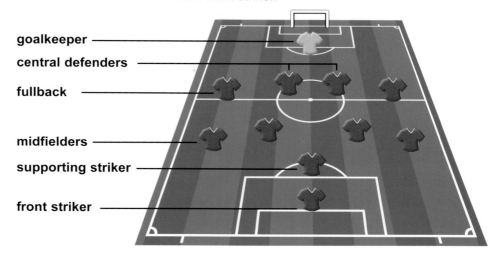

goalkeeper
central defenders
fullback
midfielders
supporting striker
front striker

3-5-2 Formation

The two wingbacks are used as wide attackers when their team has the ball, but they also play like fullbacks and drop back when their team has to defend.

wingback

4-2-3-1 Formation

This formation offers a lot of flexibility in the middle of the field. The rear row of midfielders can move back to support the defense, while the front row can move forward to support the lone striker.

Styles of Play

Within a formation, teams can play in different ways. They may place more emphasis on defense, on holding onto the ball, or making quick counterattacks. These styles of play vary during a match.

Possession and Direct Soccer

Possession soccer is when a team tries to hold onto the ball for as long as possible. Players choose easy, safe passes and rely on teammates to move into space to receive the ball. The opposition is forced to chase the ball and may tire and move out of position. This can lead to defenders leaving gaps that attackers can exploit. Rather than making lots of short, intricate passes and runs, teams playing direct soccer look to make a long pass, called a long ball, up the field. This is often aimed at a striker known as a target man.

ON THE BALL

In the 1998 World Cup, the Netherlands scored against Argentina using a long ball that looped over seven defenders before finding Dutch striker Dennis Bergkamp.

Lofted Pass

With direct soccer, the long ball is made with the instep of the shoe—this is the part of the shoe where the laces are. Here, the player is leaning back slightly so that she will get plenty of height on her pass.

Chest Control

Controlling the ball is important when receiving a long pass. This player is controlling the ball by cushioning its arrival with her chest, so that the ball drops gently in front of her feet.

Counterattack

Another style of play is counterattacking. When the other team has the ball, most of the defending players withdraw into their own half. When the defending players win the ball, they launch a rapid attack, called a counterattack. Many of their opponents will be out of position, having been on the attack themselves. This can leave spaces for the attacking team to use.

> *Everyone has their idea of what's the 'right' style. People can like the system of play or not, but that's always going to depend on the types of players you have. The most important thing is results.*
>
> England manager,
> **Fabio Capello**

Breaking Free from Defense

The team in yellow has just won possession of the ball and is counterattacking. The ball needs to be moved quickly away from the team's own goal and up the field, ahead of the opponents in blue. Teammates look to sprint forward to receive a pass.

Working Together

You do not need to have the ball to make an impact on the game. Successful players know that their movement to support teammates with the ball is still very important.

Making and Denying Space

One of the most important tasks in soccer is making space for others. At a throw-in, for instance, one attacker may run toward the teammate who is throwing in, calling loudly for the ball. This can draw a defender forward, pulling them out of position and creating space for another attacker to receive the throw. Alternatively, defenders can work as a unit to close down an attacker. The defender closest to the opponent will try to delay the attacker until support from teammates arrives.

Tactics Tip

As a defender, you should know which foot your goalkeeper prefers to kick with. When you make a backpass, it should always be to that side, so that the keeper can clear with ease.

Shepherding and Support

1 The defender (in blue) slows the attacker down without touching the attacker and giving away a foul.

2 The defender has moved, or shepherded the attacker away toward the side of the field and away from danger.

3 Even though the attacker has been able to get clear, another defender has come up in support. The attacker now has a defender in front to slow down the attack even more, and another behind to challenge him.

One-Two Move

1 The one-two is a simple and effective way of getting around defenders. Attacker number 1 makes a short pass to his teammate, attacker number 2.

2 Attacker number 1 then runs behind the defender (in yellow), who has turned toward attacker number 2. Attacker number 2 then passes back to attacker number 1.

3 Attacker number 1 now has possession of the ball and has been able to get past the defender without a challenge being made.

Supporting Possession

The player who has possession (control of the ball) relies on teammates to get into good positions to receive a pass. Players should always be aware of when a teammate gets into trouble and is under pressure from an opponent. These players can run into space and receive a short pass from their pressured teammate.

Backheel Pass

Attacker number 1 (in blue) is being challenged by a defender (in yellow). However, attacker number 2 has gotten into a good position to receive a short backheel pass. This is made with the heel of the shoe and is a good way of changing the direction of play very quickly.

Boosting the Defense

Defense is not just for defenders. The whole team can have an important role in defending, winning the ball back from the opposing team and preventing them from scoring.

Anchors and Sweepers

Some teams play with a midfield anchor who plays in front of the defense and tries to break down opposition attacks. Many other teams prefer to play the sweeper system. Here, the three or four defenders are assisted by an additional defense-minded player. As well as helping out in defense, some sweepers are also skilled at launching attacks.

Tactics Tip

Even if you are an attacker, you may still need to defend. If your coach has not told you to stay upfield, look to chase down any opposition defender with the ball, and try to pressure them into making a mistake.

Franz Beckenbauer (in white) moves past a challenger with ease. He played for West Germany from 1965–77 and turned the sweeper's role into an attacking one by bringing the ball out of defense and joining the midfield.

Sweeper Formation

Sweepers usually play slightly behind the line of defenders. From here, they can mop up any loose balls that may be heading toward the goal, or stop an opposition attack that gets past the other defenders.

sweeper —————————

defenders —————————

midfielders —————————

attackers —————————

Helping Out

During a game, a team may decide to change tactics and pull back attackers to help out the defense. For example, when the opponents have a free kick that is close to goal, the defending team's attackers often form a wall in front of the goal to stop a straightforward shot. When defending corners, a team's tallest attackers, such as France's Thierry Henry, are often brought back into their own penalty area to defend. At other times, attacking midfielders are expected to track the runs of opposing midfielders who are trying to break through the defense.

Helping in defense may involve making strong tackles. Here, Peter Ramage of the English club, Queens Park Rangers, tackles Michele Marcolini of the Italian team, Chievo Verona.

17

Defensive Tactics

Defenders will always aim to get between the ball and their goal. Usually, they will defend using one of several marking systems, such as man-marking and zonal marking.

Marking Systems

A man-marking system sees each of the defending players standing close to a particular opponent. The defenders shadow the attackers' movements, while staying between the attackers and the goal. A zonal marking system sees defending players marking areas or zones of the field. These areas overlap a little and move as the ball is moved around by the opposition team.

Defensive Marking

These defenders (in yellow) are man-marking the attacking players (in blue). The defenders will follow the attackers closely and make sure that they are always "goal side"—between the attackers they are marking and the goal.

Zonal Marking

These defenders (in red) are using zonal marking. Each zone is shown by a black box. As an attacker with the ball enters a defender's zone, the defender moves to delay the attacker, while other defenders move toward the play to help.

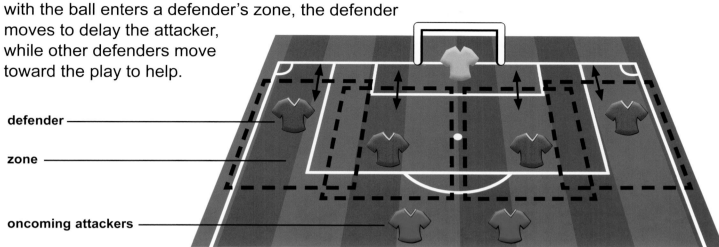

defender

zone

oncoming attackers

Mixing It Up

Sometimes, a team chooses to use zonal marking, but has one player man-marking a particularly dangerous opponent. By denying this important attacker time and space to perform, the team hopes to stop the opposition from scoring. Should they win the ball back, defenders have more decisions to make. Do they have time to move forward or are opponents close to them? If they are under pressure, defenders opt for safety first, clearing the ball a long way from their goal.

Intercepting Passes

1 Defenders should always be alert for an attacking team's mistake, which could lead to them winning back the ball. Here, a defender (in yellow) has spotted an obvious pass between two attacking players (in blue).

2 The defender runs up quickly and intercepts the pass. He now has the option of kicking the ball clear to safety or of launching an attack himself.

Attacking as a Team

Very few goals are scored by one player acting all on their own. Most are scored as a result of skillful play from teammates working well together.

Using the Width of the Field

Many teams use the tactic of filling the middle of the field with players. Other teams move players wide to the sidelines. In doing so, they can create more space between the defenders of the other team. This can lead to gaps through which attackers can run toward the goal. Alternatively, if the defenders stay quite narrow, an attacker can move down the sideline with the ball and cross it for teammates in the penalty area.

Tactics Tip

Try not to overcomplicate an attack. Do not make a long pass when a short one will do. Keep an eye out for the simplest option—it is often the best.

Creating an Overlap

1 Attacker 1 (in blue) runs behind attacker 2 to create an overlap. The defender (in yellow) moves forward to challenge attacker 2.

2 Once attacker 1 has run past the defender, attacker 2 passes to him. Attacker 1 is now clear to attack down the sideline without being challenged.

Through Ball

1 Attacker 1 has spotted a space between two defenders (in yellow). He aims a pass between the defenders. This pass is called a through ball.

2 Attacker 2 has spotted the through ball and runs behind the defense to collect the pass. He is now clear of the defense and can shoot at goal.

Overloads

When attacking, teams look for an overload—an area of the field where they have the ball and where there are more attackers than defenders. This can allow attackers to get past the defense using a one-two pass or a through ball. Good attackers also stay aware of where their teammates are in case one of them is in a better position to score a goal.

The Cutback

Sometimes, the best attacking option takes a team away from goal. The cutback is a simple attack move. It sees an attacker (shown here in blue) passing back to a teammate who is in a better shooting position.

defender

oncoming attacker

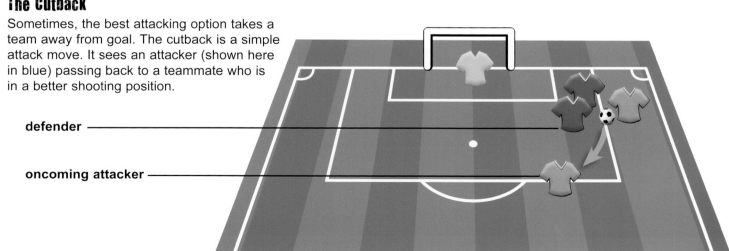

Changing Tactics

Matches do not always go according to plan and teams sometimes need to change their tactics in order to win.

Changing Players

There are many reasons why a team may alter its tactics. It may suddenly go a goal up and choose to play more defensively to protect the lead. The loss of a key player to injury or a sending off is another common reason for changing the team and its tactics.

Tactics Tip

As a player, you should always think about your opponents' strengths and weaknesses. If you spot someone who can only kick with one foot, try and force that player to use their weaker foot.

Watching for a Mismatch

This fast, skillful winger (in blue) gets past the opposing defender. She can now either cut in toward the goal or head for the goal line and put a cross into the opposition penalty area. If she did this repeatedly, the defending team's coach would have to think about changing tactics.

Exploiting Mismatches

A team's coach watches a game closely at all times, looking for mismatches where one player is struggling repeatedly with the power, pace, height, or skill of an opponent. Tactics are sometimes changed to try and cause mismatches.

One team's coach has no control over how the other team plays. They may expect their opponents to play a 4-5-1 formation only to discover the opposition going with 4-2-4. The coach may have to make changes to counter the opposition.

Choosing the Wrong Formation

Playing in the wrong formation can lead to players in certain areas of the field being outnumbered by the opposition. Here, a defender (in yellow) is facing two attackers (in blue)—with quick passing, the attackers can get around the defender easily by using a simple one-two move.

ON THE BALL

In a 2004 World Cup qualifying game against Panama, the United States coach changed tactics and brought on Eddie Johnson, who scored three goals to win the game.

Dealing with Fewer Players

With a defender sent off, this team has changed formation from 4-4-2 to 4-3-1-1. A midfielder has moved back into defense, one of the team's two strikers has dropped back to play a linking role between midfield and attack, and the two wingers have moved in to play more narrowly.

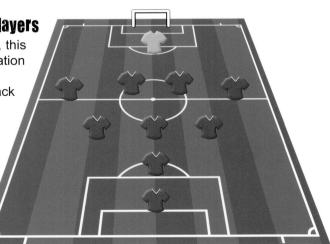

Substitutions

As well as changing formations and tactics, coaches have three other tactical tools they can use. They can issue instructions from the sidelines, they can talk to players at halftime, and they can change, or substitute players.

Substitute Numbers

As well as the starting team of players, coaches have other players, called substitutes, sitting on the bench. The number of substitutes a coach can choose from varies from competition to competition. In the English Premier League, for instance, seven players sit on the bench. From these, a coach can select up to three substitutes to bring on during a match.

ON THE BALL

During an international match against Australia in 2003, England manager Sven-Göran Eriksson substituted the entire team at halftime.

Players from the Washington Freedom (in blue) and the Philadelphia Charge (in white) compete in a WUSA women's league match in the United States. In 2001, WUSA allowed up to five substitutions during a match.

Making Substitutions

Substitutions are an important tactical tool and they are not just used to replace injured players. If a team is struggling in one area of a game, the coach might make one or more substitutions to change tactics. For example, one team may bring on a defensive midfielder when it has gone a goal up, in order to defend the lead. In contrast, the losing team might bring on an extra striker or attacking midfielder to try and score. Later on in games, many substitutions involve replacing one player with another who has the same skills and abilities. The aim is to bring on a fresh player who is not tired.

An assistant referee holds up an electronic board showing the number of the player who is to be substituted. That player then has to leave the field, and the substitute comes on.

> " *It should be 11 subs on the bench, as most squads carry a squad of 22 or 23 players. Last Saturday, we had players sitting in the stands who could have been on the bench contributing something toward the team.* "
>
> Manchester United manager,
> **Sir Alex Ferguson**

Team Spirit

Team spirit is forged on the training ground and by a team working together with a coach to achieve the same targets. However, it is also dependent on the players' determination and how committed they are to winning.

Attitude and Communication

A good team attitude starts before a match. Players should listen intently to their coach's instructions, encourage teammates, and prepare well for the game. Once out on the field, players need to keep their eyes and ears open. Listening to teammates' advice on positioning and warnings can be crucial, as can giving encouragement to a player who has just made a mistake.

ON THE BALL

In 1957, the English team, Charlton, found themselves reduced to ten men and losing 5–1 with 26 minutes to go. Even so, they ended up winning the game 7–6.

Goalkeeper

As well as guarding their goal, keepers must also organize their defenders. Here, the keeper is pointing out any gaps to his defenders and telling them where they should stand.

Captain

Team captains, such as John Terry who captains Chelsea, play an important role in keeping players' morale high. Captains should talk to and encourage their teammates and never openly criticize them.

Making a Comeback

The important thing when the other team is on top or when you are already one, two, or three goals down is not to give up. A team with good team spirit sticks together and can sometimes come back from what looks like a desperate or impossible position. During Euro 2008, Turkey found themselves 2–0 down against the Czech Republic with just 16 minutes left. However, they did not give up and managed to score three goals in the time remaining, winning the game 3–2.

Tactics Tip

Never ease up when your team is in the lead, even if it seems your team is far better than the opposition. It takes only a second to score a goal and many major teams have been embarrassed by a "lesser" team fighting back and winning.

Xabi Alonso of Liverpool celebrates scoring the equalizing goal during the 2005 Champions League Final. Liverpool had been 3–0 down at halftime to the Italian team AC Milan, but went on to tie the game and then win on penalties.

Set-Piece Tactics

Set pieces are ways of restarting the game after the ball has left the field or a foul has occurred. Teams practice them regularly because they often lead to goals.

Throw-ins and Corners

Throw-ins may seem unthreatening, but a good team can turn them into an attacking weapon. Some teams have a player who can make long throws into the opposition penalty area. Corners are awarded when a defender is the last to touch the ball before it rolls over the goal line.

Tactics Tip

To make a free kick or corner work, you may need to get free of an opponent marking you. Drop one shoulder and lean one way as if you are about to sprint in one direction, before pushing off hard and sprinting in the opposite direction.

Types of Corner

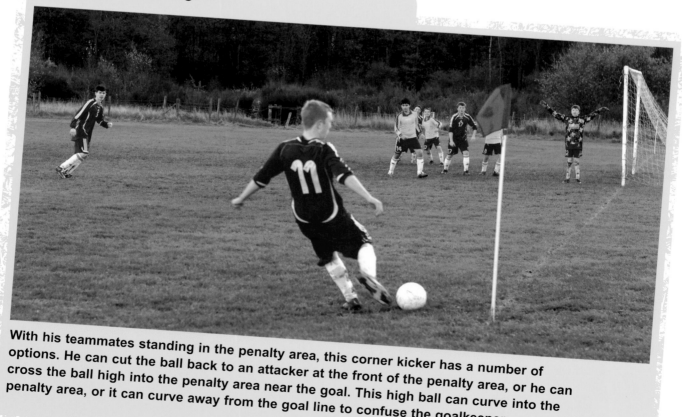

With his teammates standing in the penalty area, this corner kicker has a number of options. He can cut the ball back to an attacker at the front of the penalty area, or he can cross the ball high into the penalty area near the goal. This high ball can curve into the penalty area, or it can curve away from the goal line to confuse the goalkeeper.

Free Kicks

Free kicks are awarded when the opposition has committed an offense, such as a foul. Some free kicks are taken quickly to get the ball moving and to try to trick opponents, while others take some time. Teams will practice various free kick moves, including passing to another teammate who can shoot at goal from a different angle or using a dummy runner.

Side Pass

1 Rather than shooting directly at goal, the side pass free kick sees attacker 1 making a short pass to attacker 2, who is standing to one side.

2 In doing so, attacker 2 now has a clear shot at the goal, without the wall of defenders (in yellow) standing in front of him.

Dummy Runner

1 In this type of free kick, attacker 1 runs up to the ball as if he is going to take the free kick. Attacker 2 waits behind him.

2 Instead of kicking the ball, attacker 1 steps over it. Attacker 2 then runs up behind attacker 1.

3 Attacker 2 shoots, aiming away from the keeper, who has been fooled by the dummy runner and has committed himself in the wrong direction.

What It Takes To Be...

A Top Coach

Jose Mourinho

Mourinho's father, Felix, was a soccer coach, and as a teenager, Jose watched his father's training sessions. Mourinho studied sports science in Portugal and brought a scientific attitude to training and tactics in his first jobs at several small Portuguese clubs, before working at bigger clubs such as Barcelona in Spain. He developed his own tactics as coach of Barcelona's B team, before enjoying success at Porto in Portugal and Chelsea in England. In 2008, he was appointed head coach of Internazionale in Italy.

Career Path

- ⚽ 1992: Took a job as a translator at Sporting Lisbon in Portugal.

- ⚽ 1996: Moved to Barcelona.

- ⚽ 2000: Became head coach of Benfica in Portugal.

  2002: Appointed head coach of Porto.

- ⚽ 2004: Won Champions League with Porto.

- ⚽ 2004: Was Chelsea manager.

- ⚽ 2008: Appointed manager of Serie A club Internazionale.

Mourinho won the Portuguese League twice and the Champions League when he was coach of Porto. He also coached Chelsea to two Premier League titles.

Glossary

coach someone who works with the players, deciding who should play and what tactics to use. They do not get involved in any business aspects of the soccer club.

counterattack when defenders win back possession of the ball and launch a quick attack before the opposition players can organize their defense.

fullback a defender who plays mainly on the sides of the field.

game changers players who are so skillful that they can alter the course of a match.

heart rate the number of times your heart beats in a minute.

manager someone who oversees the running of the team, deciding which players play and what tactics to use, and gets involved in the business decisions, such as which players to buy and sell.

midfielders the players who play in the central part of the field.

possession soccer a style of play where players make short passes to each other, keeping possession of the ball.

season the continuous run of games over an entire year.

striker a team's best goal scorer and the player who usually plays nearest the opposition goal.

teamwork when players work together as a unit rather than as individuals.

wingback a midfield player who plays wide along the sides of the field.

Further Reading

Soccer Skills
by Clive Gifford (Kingfisher, 2005)

Soccer Skills For Young Players
by Ted Buxton (Firefly Books, 2007)

The Everything Kids' Soccer Book
by Deborah W Orisfield
(Adams Media, 2009)

Web Sites

Due to the changing nature of Internet links, PowerKids Press has developed an online list of Web sites related to the subject of this book. This site is updated regularly. Please use this link to access this list:
http://www.powerkidslinks.com/sos/team

Index